MULTIFACE(T)S

Style Yourself with Jewelry

SWAROVSKI

Creative direction
Nathalie Colin
Yamila Tandeau de Marsac

Project leader
Allison Pyrah

Project coordinator
MarjanTharin

Iconographer
Yamila Tandeau de Marsac

ÉDITIONS
DE LA MARTINIÈRE

Graphic designer
Florine Synoradzki

Editor
Nathalie Chapuis

Image research
Sandrine Vincent
Marie Poussade

Copy editing
JMS Books LLP

ABRAMS

Cataloging-in-Publication Data has been
applied for and may be obtained from
the Library of Congress.

ISBN: 978-1-4197-0769-8

Published in 2013 by Abrams, an imprint
of ABRAMS. All rights reserved. No portion
of this book may be reproduced, stored in
a retrieval system, or transmitted in any form
or by any means, mechanical, electronic,
photocopying, recording, or otherwise, without
written permission from the publisher.

Printed and bound in Italy

10 9 8 7 6 5 4 3 2 1

Abrams books are available at special
discounts when purchased in quantity
for premiums and promotions as well as
fundraising or educational use. Special
editions can also be created to specification.
For details, contact:
specialsales@abramsbooks.com
or the address below.

ABRAMS
THE ART OF BOOKS SINCE 1949

115 West 18th Street
New York, NY 10011
www.abramsbooks.com

SWAROVSKI

MULTIFACE(T)S
Style Yourself with Jewelry

by Nathalie Colin

– text by Laetitia Wajnapel –

SWAROVSKI

Abrams | New York

"*Growing up as a child, I was constantly surrounded by crystal, and from a young age I was fascinated by its beauty and its power to make people smile. Now, with children of my own, I enjoy watching the radiance of crystal having the same effect on them. When sparkling crystal is transformed into a piece of jewelry, it takes on a whole new dimension, as it becomes an integral part of the woman who wears it, and that same sparkle emanates from her, bringing out that smile wherever she goes.*"

Robert Buchbauer
Member of the Executive Board and Swarovski family member

Being the Creative Director of the Swarovski House provides me with the fantastic opportunity to bring to their collections a richness of style and a creative diversity—supported in this mission by the visionary influence of Robert Buchbauer. The multifaceted character of my work and my passion for accessories have always lured me to explore new territories of expression.

The democratization of jewelry is at the origin of the brand's DNA, a heritage perpetuated with each new season. The contemporary nature of the designs abolishes the barriers of traditional wearability, breaking free from passing diktats, and avoids the monotony of the "total look," favoring instead the fusion of geographic and cultural frontiers.

In creating this book, I wanted to share the effervescence of style ideas that flood the design studio daily, and that of leading professionals—key figures in the world of fashion—notably Nina Garcia, Glenda Bailey, Anna Dello Russo, and Eric Daman. My profound thanks to them all for their enlightened points of view. During our animated discussions, Laetitia Wajnapel managed to find the right words to reflect and translate my creative vision. Guest designers June Ambrose, Sascha Lilic, and Frankie Han showed great audacity in their fusion of accessories and garments for the exclusive fashion series shot in New York, Paris, and Hong Kong.

How do I complete a look with the perfect jewelry? How do I add a touch of brilliance, the signature of my individuality? In what contexts should one choose a minimalist look . . . or on the contrary, a layered one? How do you have fun with jewelry and make the most of its versatility? How do you find the perfect alchemy between personal expression and timeless references? Bearing in mind a desire for accessibility and with the aim of covering a wide range of styles, this book offers page after page of innovative ideas, allowing for a rich dialogue between jewelry, garment, and body.

I hope that every reader will appreciate the optimistic, eclectic, sincere, and sometimes playful spirit that guides this publication, allowing women to cultivate their own unique look, have fun with accessories, and bring out the various aspects of their personality. My warm thanks to women who, every day, fascinate and inspire me through their ability to metamorphose—with inimitable grace and brilliance!

CON

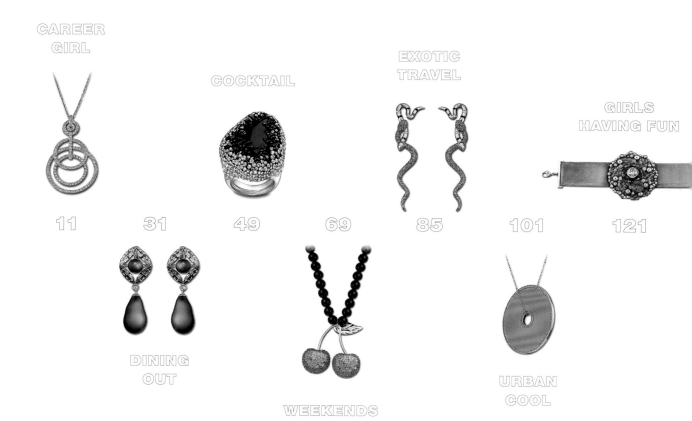

TENTS

CLUBBING

RENDEZ-
VOUS

WEDDING

139   155   169   185   199   213

EXPRESS
YOURSELF

READY
TO ROCK

CELEBRATION

CAREER GIRL

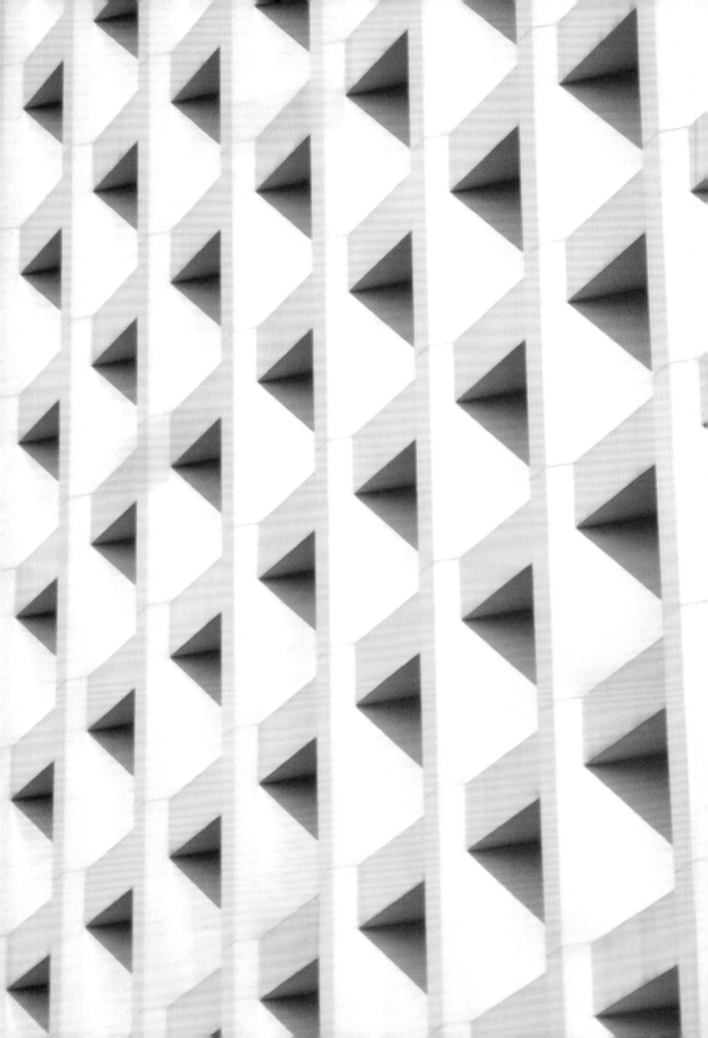

Sitting at a desk over eight hours a day can be a true style challenge, especially if a smart dress code is enforced in your office. Playing around with the "trimmings" is a good way to break up a possibly boring sartorial routine. Different shirts or colored tights will definitely come in handy to jazz up your work wear. You can also rely on jewelry to make a difference.

FIRST IMPRESSION

The first impression is often the only one, so make sure you always look and act your very best.

The classic Nirvana ring is a great ally when you want to make a big impression. It is the ultimate statement piece, with its strong lines and pure shape. It's a ring that speaks for itself, so wear it on its own and let your hands do the talking.

"I'm a strong, powerful woman and when I wear big jewelry, particularly bracelets and rings, I feel powerful, expressive, and at the same time feminine, because the impressive size of the jewelry balances out my own strong shape, making me feel taller and more delicate in contrast."

Brisa Roche

Another trick to make an impression is to play on geometric shapes in black and white or black and navy. The effect is very powerful while staying classic and understated. It will give you an air of authority.

It's important not to allow your personality to disappear behind your work clothes. Adopting a formal style or wearing a suit doesn't mean you should forget about your personality. Find ways to make formal work for you and let yourself shine.

Play on asymmetry and wear all your jewelry on one side only.... Don't lose your balance though!

Match your necklace to your skir

Size does matter: if you are a junior, keep it fresh with a small necklace, or earn some respect with one that makes a statement.

BE YOURSELF

"I usually do not dress down for business. On the contrary, cocktail rings, big cuffs, and opulent necklaces help boost my self-confidence!"

Nathalie Colin

and add a subtle hint of color. If it matches your Post-it Notes, it's even better....

Five Ways To Wear Your White Shirt

Button it up to the top and wear a short necklace (or a brooch) under the collar.

Open a couple of buttons and cover up with a short multi-strand necklace worn under the shirt. Tuck your shirt into some black pants.

Use your shirt as a jacket, worn over a simple tee shirt, and wear a classic pendant around the neck.

Wear a fitted shirt, unbuttoned quite low, with a vintage-inspired necklace and a pencil skirt for a sexy fifties look.

Double up your necklaces and tuck a boyfriend shirt into a leather skirt if you feel like a rock chick.

DRESS YOUR DECOLLETAGE!

If you are petite

Stand out from the crowd by wearing a large, sparkly, baroque medallion on a thin chain. Don't wear it too low on your chest though.

If you are tall

Try to focus attention on your upper half to balance out your height. Accessorize as much as you like; choose a covering plastron necklace.

If you have a large bust

Less is more! Play on the subtlety of a single emerald drop. Use your décolletage to show off this delicate pendant.

If you are flat chested

Wear several strand necklaces of various lengths, including sparkling contemporary beads for a large, fluid, bib effect.

If you have a long neck

Go for the opulent choker. Dress your neck with larger pieces to balance out its length.

If you have a short neck

Try a tiny solitaire pendant for a delicate, minimalist look.

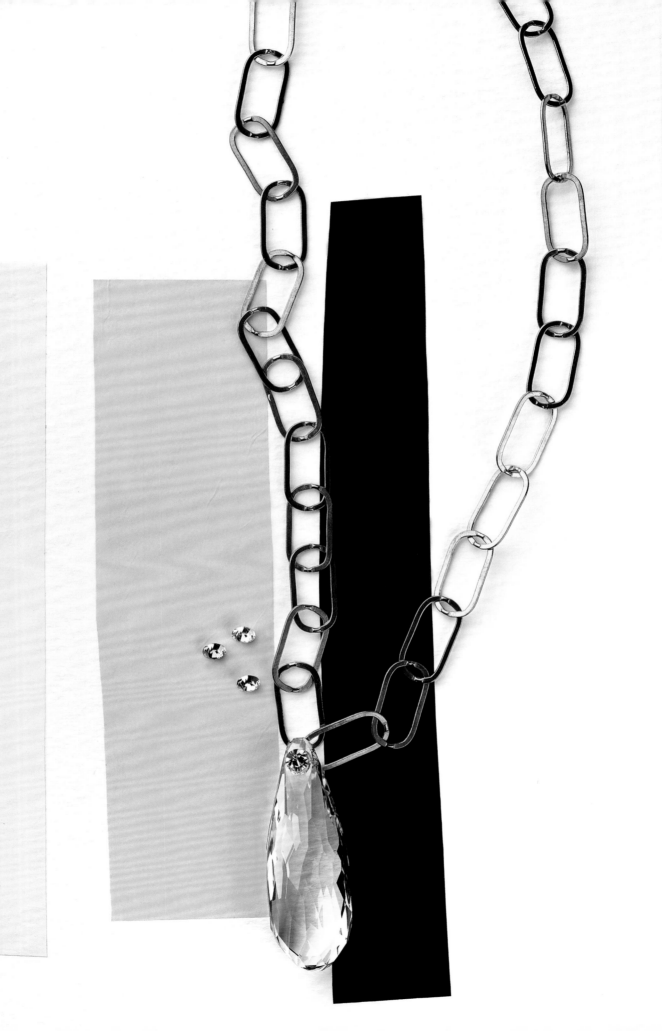

Create a makeshift jewelry box in your desk drawer at work. Make room between the paperclips, pens, and Post-it Notes for an extension of your wardrobe. This will be your "work-to-cocktail hour" emergency kit. It should contain a few brooches to pin on your jacket, some stud earrings for your buttonholes, small chandelier earrings, a cocktail ring or two, and maybe even a few ornate cuffs and bangles. If you want to be extra prepared, you could even keep a spare shirt or jacket in your office, something a little more fashionable than regular work attire.

Break up formal black with shades of rose-gold and nude.

When you travel for business, you have to be ready for any type of situation... with only a limited wardrobe.

TRAVEL IN STYLE

If you are due to speak at a conference, make sure you don't wear too many bangles as the jingling sound will distract from what you are saying. Avoid long necklaces too, as they will interfere with radio microphones.

"In the daytime, your hands take the lead, but at night it is all about your face. Be smart and play with the versatility of transition jewelry."

Nathalie Colin

DAY to NIGHT

The main difference between working hours and the cocktail hour is where you want to put the focus.

During the day, a simple necklace will brighten up a black outfit.

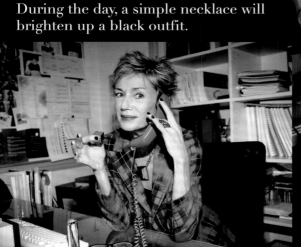

At night, shift the focus to your face with earrings.

"I really like bracelets and rings, maybe because they are worn on your hand, and you have a sense of power that is close to you, your everyday life and your movements."

Berenice Marlohe

Don't be too hasty to reject formal dress code — it may offer some extra style options for evening wear. There is nothing quite so cool as a classic with a twist. Think of the possibilities hidden in your skirt suit! Think of how much fun it will be to play around with to make it cocktail-friendly!

No matter what your life is like, what you do for a living or which social circles you tend to hover in, there is one occasion that invariably sends any woman I know into a frenzy: the chic dinner party. Not just any old dinner party, THE dinner party to end all dinner parties, something so stylish and sophisticated that even Grace Kelly would have a panic attack.

"I hate rules, and for me there is not a particular jewel for an evening gala or a special night. The only dress code I can suggest is: In front of Queen Elizabeth, it's better to leave your jewels at home. The Queen's jewels are THE jewels."

Anna dello Russo

MONO-CHROME

COLOR PALETTE Look for jewelry that is multifaceted, while keeping the palette as close as possible to monochrome or a subtle camaieu. Whether you prefer warm or cool colors is up to you.

EVENING WEAR DOESN'T MEAN "BLACK" Don't hesitate to wear color when you go out for dinner. If you don't want to rush into it, try monochrome outfits and wear different shades of the same color. You can either clash or match your accessories.

Despite its glamorous appeal and the promise of fine food, elegant dresses, and sparkling jewelry, a dinner party can be quite an ordeal style-wise. Let's imagine it's taking place on a Saturday night, so you have all the time in the world to get ready (make that fifteen minutes if you have children). Remember you will spend most of the evening sitting down, so it is your upper body that needs the most attention. My main advice is: when in doubt, choose the little black dress. But let me throw in one other piece of advice that comes from the heart. When food is involved, avoid the close-fitting little black dress. You will thank me later!

DECOLLETE

Strapless

For extra visual effect,
add a long pendant
or chain.

Open shirt

Loosen the rigid
structure of
a shirt by wearing
a soft asymmetrical
necklace.

*"It is important to work on your cleavage.
A nice V-neck with a pretty, dangling pendant
quivering on the skin suggests sensual
things that are to come."*

Nathalie Colin

Deep V-neck

Wear two or three
necklaces of different
lengths and shapes,
starting with a ribbon
choker.

Round
neck tee

Give it a
contemporary look
with a scarf necklace.

Halterneck

Wear a short, ornate necklace to give the illusion of an embroidered neckline.

Short V-neck

Follow the collar with a short, simple V-shaped necklace.

Boatneck

This is a tricky one, so just wear a very large medallion on a short, simple chain.

Cowl-neck

Play with the draping and wear two or three necklaces over it so that they get lost in the fabric.

ROUND COLLAR
Wear a collar-shaped, bejeweled necklace to create the illusion of embroidery.

ASYMMETRIC
Wear a crystal cuff on your non-watch arm for a striking effect.

LITTLE BLACK DRESS

A little black dress is every girl's first choice when time is tight. But it doesn't have to be boring. Here are four ways to style it.

PLAIN LONG SLEEVES
Play on the contrast between a rather austere dress, extravagant cocktail rings, and a crystal watch.

STRAPLESS
How about an exquisite choker or chandelier earrings?

If your little black dress has a revealing neckline, try on opulent Y necklace. While it will definitely draw attention to you, it will also conveniently distract people from staring at your décolletage.

Sequins should not necessarily prevent you from accessorizing. Keep the rest of your outfit plain and try wearing a few chain necklaces.

"For a dinner party, I would rather choose spectacular chandelier earrings or a necklace that will add a touch of sparkle around my face. When styling with jewelry, you have to be strategic and at dinner parties your face (and the conversation) must be the center of attention."

Nathalie Colin

Black and white is a great styling trick for dinner parties. Make it your signature style for the evening.

Contrast textures and colors, such as pearls with a shagreen effect, for a contemporary look.

BLACK
&
WHITE

Black and white is reminiscent of Art Deco style. Think strong, graphic shapes.

Don't shy away from very ornate pieces; they are a great complement to an understated dinner outfit, such as the little black dress. While you want to keep the focus on the upper half of your body and frame your face, you can match the colors of your earrings to your clutch bag for example. Being color coordinated is absolutely fine, but you want to do it in a subtle way.

"I love statement pieces of jewelry and I like to wear dramatic styles—like my trademark Nirvana ring—every day."

Nadja Swarovski

*"My must-have is a cocktail ring. It adds
an exclamation mark to your look."*

Nina Garcia

Parties are a little like
the Olympics. You can't just
show up and expect to shine,
even if you are covered in
diamonds from head to toe.
You need to be prepared.
To begin with, you need
to have a clear idea of what
the evening has in store:
Is it an art opening?
Is it a party at a friend's house?
An awards ceremony?

"I am a real chameleon when it comes to evening wear. I think going out is a great time to let your imagination run wild. So dare, dare, and dare! Explore new ways of styling yourself with less predictable looks. Explore, have fun, and become one of the most wanted guests who always brings a sense of freshness to a cocktail party."

Nathalie Colin

CONVERSATION PIECE

Use jewelry to break the ice.

The ideal conversation piece lies somewhere between clothing and jewelry. You want to blur boundaries and get people talking.

If you are going to a house party, why not wear that vintage prom dress you keep in the closet for special occasions? Just add some sculptural heels and really edgy jewelry. How about a full sleeve and a shoulder piece embroidered with crystals? Or a princess necklace to make your dress even more couture? If your dress has three-quarter sleeves, try wearing two or three cuff bracelets on one arm for a futuristic effect. It will contrast nicely with the primness of the prom dress.

ON THE BACK

Have you thought about turning things upside down and wearing your necklace back to front? Admittedly it works best with backless dresses. The front of your outfit can be as minimalistic as you like, as long as you make sure people will talk about you behind your back as you leave the room. Literally!

You are off to the opening of a hot new artist in a cool but derelict loft in a super trendy area. Your outfit should be simple, such as a silk camisole with jeans and a blazer, paired with open-toed shoe boots. Let your accessories do the talking. Pin a few vintage-inspired brooches really high on the shoulders of your blazer so that they look like epaulettes, for a military look, and add a long rope necklace that makes your camisole cling subtly to your skin. Wear as many cocktail rings as you can on just one finger or go for an articulated ring.

DOUBLE UP

Why wear only one
necklace when you
could wear two?
Match or clash,
it's up to you.

BANGLE MANIA

Turn your bangle collection into your own couture piece.

Wear several bangles together, for example, wear three large ones on one arm, or two on each. Make a cuff by wearing three bangles together.

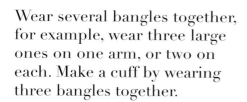

"A woman's power is stated through her jewelry. A woman would never venture into public without her adornments, giving her the power to confront the world as if wearing armor. An amazon carrying her shield."

Barbara Berger

If you already have the ultimate dress for an awards ceremony, all you need now is something to add the finishing touch, the glitz to go with the glamour. While your necklace, earrings, and bracelets can remain fairly subdued, you can still shake things up a little with a crystal clutch bag.

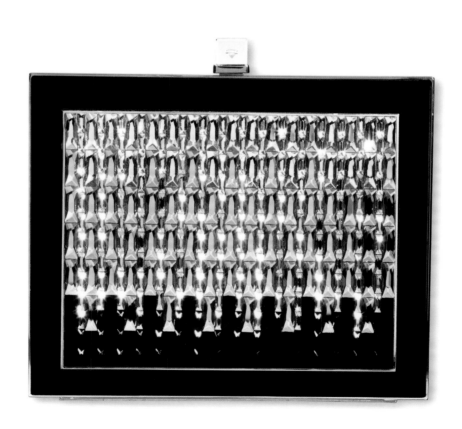

"Just remember: Don't apologize, accessorize!"

Eric Daman

WEEK-
ENDS

When we talk about "casual" wear, the first thing that comes to mind is the all-American uniform: blue jeans and white tee. It evokes freedom from social pressures and conventions, but also a fuss-free approach to personal style.

A TOUCH OF SPARKLE

Don't keep your shiny things hidden away at the weekend!
A figurative pendant is more sophisticated with a few sparkles. Give your outfit some chic accents with pieces that sparkle subtly. It's fine to wear resin jewelry at the weekend, but make sure it has a little twist, such as rhinestones or silver accents; anything goes as long as it shines.

"When I meet up with friends for the weekend, I choose some small but lovely earrings to dress myself up, cheer myself up, and generally brighten myself up!"

Shu Qi

Casualness is about showing who we are rather than what we do. When our occupation doesn't dictate what we wear, self-expression takes center stage.

Clothes become a blank canvas, ready to be embellished in a way that helps define our personality, which is why jewelry needs to be chosen very carefully. Picking pieces to go with casual outfits is a truly organic process. Everything has to feel just right and fall into place naturally, like a second skin.

CASUAL CLASH

Mix textures for a refined, sophisticated look: warm with cold, soft with hard. A beautiful piece of knitwear takes on a whole new dimension when worn with some stunning jewelry.

"As a French woman, I do not allow myself to dress down when I go out, even to buy a baguette on a Saturday morning. My banker or the man of my dreams may just be around the corner, about to be charmed or horrified. The trick is to wear stylish accessories (jewels and shoes) that will always ensure the most 'effortless' look!!!"

Nathalie Colin

Whether it is a single statement pendant on a long chain or a multitude of small, dainty necklaces contrasting with a knitted top, casual jewelry is soft, serene, and completes us. This doesn't mean everything has to look "Zen." On the contrary it can be as zesty as we are, but it must feel like it is another limb, a part of ourselves that we couldn't leave the house without. Think of it like perfume—on the days that you rushed to get ready on time and forgot to spray a tiny bit of familiar scent on your wrists or behind your ears, didn't you feel exposed, naked?

It is almost the same deep-rooted relationship we have with our casual jewelry.

*"Feeling glamorous but your style is more casual?
Try layering two or three chunky and sparkly necklaces
on top of each other with a simple tee or cosy sweater."*

Eric Daman

SIMPLY SERENE

When looking for inner peace, sometimes the easiest thing to do is to open your jewelry box.

"Nature is my inspiration. Its organic forms have always been the starting point for creation. Women should always wear simple clothes and jewelry inspired by nature, because…. True beauty is nature in its purest form."

Oscar Carvallo

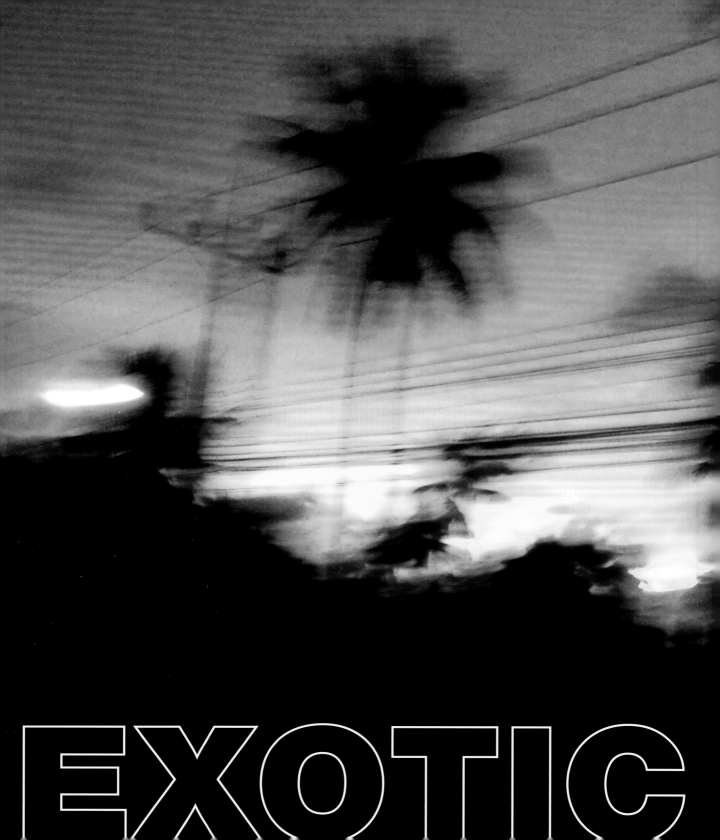

TRAVEL

Ah, the vacation, that blissful week or two that you have waited so long for, but which is often preceded by a packing panic so frantic that it can ruin the first few days of your vacation. Packing is mostly about deciding on a vacation persona. Once you have made your decision, go through your wardrobe and think about each item as a piece in a puzzle.

"I usually follow the seasons rather than the mood of the day. During summer I love wearing colored jewels, and during the colder seasons, more neutral ones."

Cristina Chiaboto

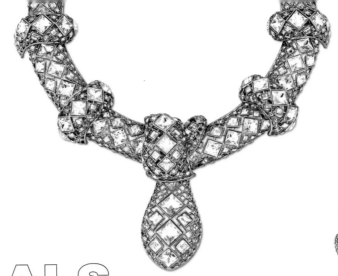

ANIMALS

Jewelry based on or inspired by reptiles is a great way to add a bit of edge to an outfit.

A snake winding itself around your finger is both striking and evocative of both danger and passion, but also something very sensual.

"I love traveling and have been to many countries. Every time I am in a different place, I love to buy some jewelry and accessories from the local culture."

Zhang Zi Lin

ETHNIC MIX

Mix and match jewelry brought back from your travels abroad with ethnic-inspired pieces for a cool, modern style.

Friendship bracelets are great; if you wear one by itself, it will be a constant reminder of your fun-filled teenage years. Alternatively, wear several at once for instant fashion kudos.

Each piece of jewelry should "connect" with at least three others, so everything else you pack should follow the same rule. Spend a few days selecting your outfits carefully. Don't leave it till the last minute to avoid total packing meltdown. Pack your jewelry in a large silk pouch, but keep it with you in your cabin bag, never check it in. Finally, avoid wearing too much jewelry when you fly.

At last you are on the beach, doing whatever it is that you do on vacation. You open the silk pouch you filled with jewelry and what do you find? None of your usual pieces! Diamonds and rubies are not vacation appropriate. It is time to go ethnic—wooden beads and semiprecious stones will fit the bill instead. Choose warm tones or a palette of whites to set off a bronzed summer skin. And rather than covering up your tummy and hips with a sarong, wear several sets of colorful beads around your neck and walk tall. Everyone will focus on your accessorizing skills rather than any defects in your figure.

TRIBAL SOUL

Give an urban twist to your jewelry by combining wood and crystals.

Wooden jewelry gets a facelift!

Look for metal jewelry combined with ethnic-inspired prints—African and ikat designs are always popular.

"I find different and interesting pieces of jewelry when I travel, especially beautiful pieces from Africa."

Ariadne Artiles

"Asia is my favorite destination for vacation, at least once a year. I always take home one set of white jewels which looks wonderful on tanned skin. Coral and yellow are also good colors to really highlight the skin in summer."

Nathalie Colin

URBAN
COOL

The most inspiring things are not in magazines, on TV or in books. They are all right in front of you in the street. You don't need a fashion magazine to tell you which color will be in this season, you just need to look around you at all the vibrant colors leaping out from the gray urban mass. Street culture permeates all aspects of life, including fashion. Style on the street is about self-expression and fun, practicality and individuality at the same time. Denim, cotton, and jersey, in bold colors and prints, are your best allies. If you feel more Earth Mother than hip-hop sister, go for muted tones and silky fabrics, mixed with denim and some knitwear.

Denim is
a timeless and
transgenerational
fabric. Give it
a more urban twist
by pairing it with
colorful jewelry.

DENIM CULTURE

Take no prisoners, clash colors, wear large brooches—anything goes with denim.

FUN KNITS

Slouchy knits can be oh so nonchalantly sexy when worn with the right accessories.

When picking accessories to go with knitwear, choose long, fluid necklaces, or try several necklaces and bracelets together. Mix metallic and colorful rubber watches. Who said knitwear was stuffy?

As far as jewelry goes, the motto is always the same: Bold is beautiful. A simple gray sweatshirt is worn with knee-high socks and a bib necklace. Jeans are paired with a leather jacket. Bangles and rings echo the zips on the jacket. If you wear a printed top, think about the stir you'd create when matching it with the right accessories.

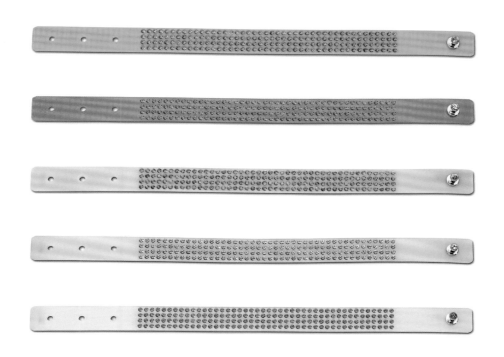

GRAPHIC PLAY

Make it a rule to buy pieces of jewelry in several different colorways, then mix them all up.

One really sparkling cocktail ring can liven up a whole outfit.

Design by
Pedro Lourenço

By stacking a few identical bangles in different colors, you can create an interesting striped effect—very graphic. Play on colors, materials, and textures for a really fresh look.

"What I find most fascinating is the relationship between skin, clothes, and jewelry. Tattoo art is about intimacy and exposure at the same time; about hiding and revealing, and so is urban cool jewelry. … Telling stories with written messages and figurative symbols. The mix of jewels makes each story unique and strongly reveals individuality."

Nathalie Colin

Don't shy away from wearing jewelry if your clothes have zips. On the contrary, use the zips too—accessorize them with chains, bracelets, and rings.

PAINT IT BLACK

Black is the go-to color for an edgy, urban look. Black doesn't mean plain.

Your jewelry tells its own tale. Pair up figurative pieces to recount little stories and scenarios.

If you are in a sporty mood, a bomber jacket will look great with rolled up sleeves, colorful leather gloves, and a large, gold cuff.

You may as well start using the crystal-decorated bag you were keeping for the Oscars (since your invitation seems to have got lost in the post), but rather than glamming it up, try dressing it down with a jersey maxi dress and some sneakers. If you do, keep the rest of your accessories simple to balance it out. Remember styling, and especially jewelry styling, is about balance. Nothing needs to match, but there should be a good balance.

GIRLS

HAVING FUN

In 1998, something really special happened to girlfriends all over the world.... A TV show, called *Sex and the City*, gave girl time the ultimate validation. Women everywhere spent hours wondering if they were a Carrie, Charlotte, Samantha or Miranda. So what if we don't all have a shoe collection to rival Imelda Marcos and a townhouse on Park Avenue? We can still meet up for brunch and dissect our current relationships!

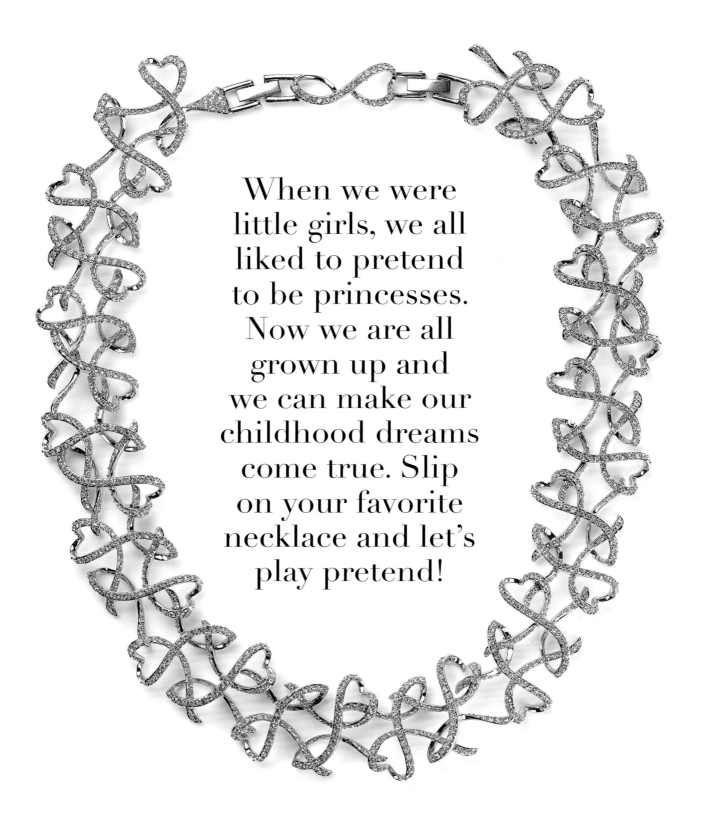

When we were
little girls, we all
liked to pretend
to be princesses.
Now we are all
grown up and
we can make our
childhood dreams
come true. Slip
on your favorite
necklace and let's
play pretend!

YOU ARE A PRINCESS

A tiara is a fun over-the-top accessory that adds just a little touch of sparkle in your hair.
Time to adopt the princess necklace, an all-around necklace made using very classic techniques.

Wear an exceptional piece of jewelry for a drink with friends.
Cocktail rings, extravagant bangles, anything goes.

PLAY WITH PRINTS

Whoever said "less is more" obviously never had fun with prints. Embrace your maximalist side.

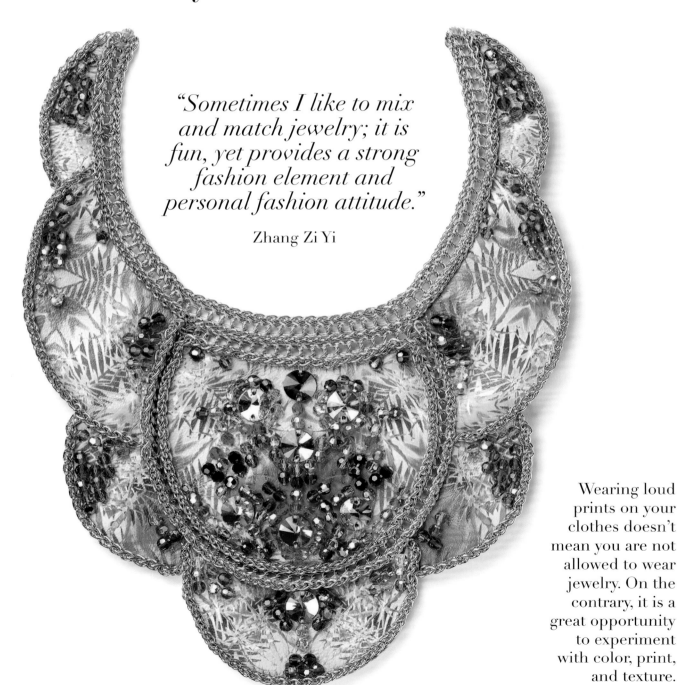

"Sometimes I like to mix and match jewelry; it is fun, yet provides a strong fashion element and personal fashion attitude."

Zhang Zi Yi

Wearing loud prints on your clothes doesn't mean you are not allowed to wear jewelry. On the contrary, it is a great opportunity to experiment with color, print, and texture.

> *"My biggest style rule applies also to jewelry: Have fun with it. Be fearless, and always do the unexpected."*
>
> Nina Garcia

MESSAGES

When wearing a figurative ring, always make sure it is turned toward the person you are talking to. For example, a heart-shaped ring should have the tip of the heart pointing toward your fingernails.

We also share a very special bond with the magician who gave birth to us. We all have childhood memories involving our mother's jewelry collection, or her closet full of fascinating things. Remember stroking her precious evening dresses, or trying to walk in her high heels? Or perhaps you liked to wear all her necklaces at the same time and pretend you were a pirate?

Wear jewelry that is round during pregnancy, such as a circular pendant that you can caress to enter a Zen-like state.

Or a pendant containing loose stones that move around inside it, calming and relaxing you.

You can also play with symbolism and wear a stone inside a stone as a metaphor for maternity.

MOTHER & DAUGHTER

Celebrate the most special bond in your life.

Things may be different now.... You may be the one watching in wonder as your own child ransacks your bedroom in her quest for dressing-up clothes. Or you may enjoy the moments you spend with your mother, bonding over an afternoon of coffee, patisseries, and shopping. Now you are both adults, you can share jewelry properly, or even go shopping for new jewelry together.

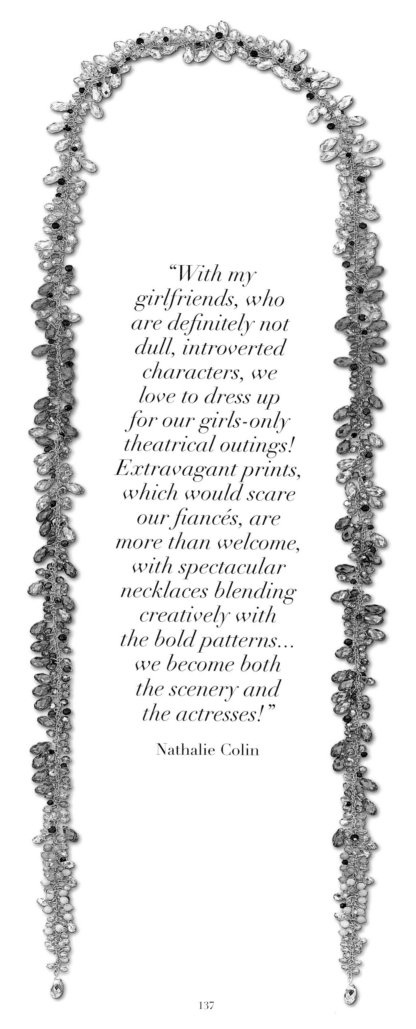

"With my girlfriends, who are definitely not dull, introverted characters, we love to dress up for our girls-only theatrical outings! Extravagant prints, which would scare our fiancés, are more than welcome, with spectacular necklaces blending creatively with the bold patterns... we become both the scenery and the actresses!"

Nathalie Colin

XPRESS
URSELF

Expressing yourself is a daily struggle. We all want our personality to shine through our clothes; we want to transcend the trends, to forget about the catwalks, and to be free from the dictates of fashion while remaining super stylish in our own way.

DRESS IN JEWELS

Being yourself is all about finding ways to make the clothes you wear look as unique as you are.

"Jewelry worn with accessories and clothing is one of the main tools for expressing creativity and kookiness in everyday life."

Ara Stark

Whether you opt for a few simple pieces that have very special memories for you, or decide to wear several items together in order to make a statement, the way you wear jewelry says more about you than what you are wearing.

"Jewelry is not just a frivolous embellishment on a woman, but a statement of refined taste. Imagine Chanel without her pearls, Lacroix without the gold . . . it would be like a nice dinner without any salt or spices."

Sascha Lilic

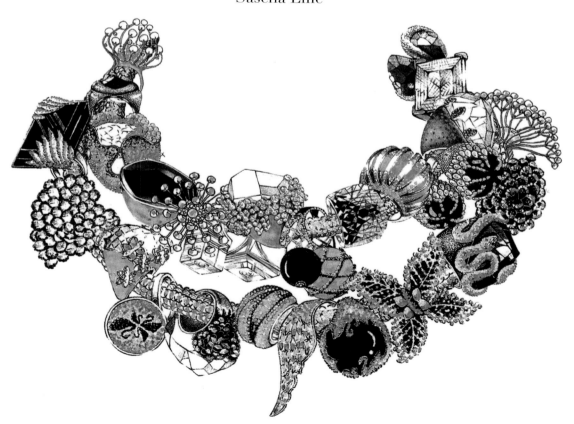

MATCH YOUR MAKEUP

Think about the harmony between makeup and jewelry and make your accessories an extension of your beauty regime. Match colors, shapes . . . Have fun!

"The ring is such a multi-talented piece of jewelry! It can express the mood you are in, your social status, your style, and at the same time underline each of your gestures."

Sascha Lilic

WATCH YOUR WATCH!

Of all the pieces of jewelry you own, your watch is probably the one that gets the most wear. It is possibly also the only one you actually rely on. But what jewelry should you wear with your watch? Here are a few combinations.

"I love the old-fashioned allure of a classic bracelet watch. It feels so nostalgic and right in the iPhone-as-clock era."

Glenda Bailey

Much in the same way that you let your personality shine through your clothes, you can let your jewelry shine through too. A very large, sparkly necklace camouflaged beneath a sheer top makes a unique statement about who you are and how you lead your life. It is about revealing what you want, when you want to. It is about taking control of your life.

*"Express yourself is the main 'motto'
of my life, and even of my job.
But there is no single way to do this.
I believe there is more than one life for
us out there, more than one career, more
than one life path, more than one dream
to realize, more than one city to live in,
several chances to meet the man of your
dreams. So many ways to express our
multifaceted personalities, and definitely
more than one jewelry style with which
to do so!!!"*

Nathalie Colin

Traditionally, the night is a dark place where demons come out and take over while we sleep, so it is quite logical for dress codes to loosen up a lot when darkness falls. Clubs are strange places where we go to get lost in the music and forget our humdrum daily lives. We've all experienced the womb-like trance of being pressed against dozens of strangers on a strobe-lit dance floor while hypnotic music pulsates in the background.

*"Jewels are for me
the ultimate accessory.
They brighten up my looks
at my parties around
the world."*

Cathy Guetta

GROOVY JEWELS

In the dim light of a club, jewelry takes on a life of its own. It shimmers, sashays, and undulates around your neck like a waterfall. Choose crystal mesh accessories on club nights; they will follow your every move and reflect light in the most magical way.

"A look is never complete without a few great pieces of jewelry. It helps me to translate the look and tell the story. It's bling that makes a look sing!"

June Ambrose

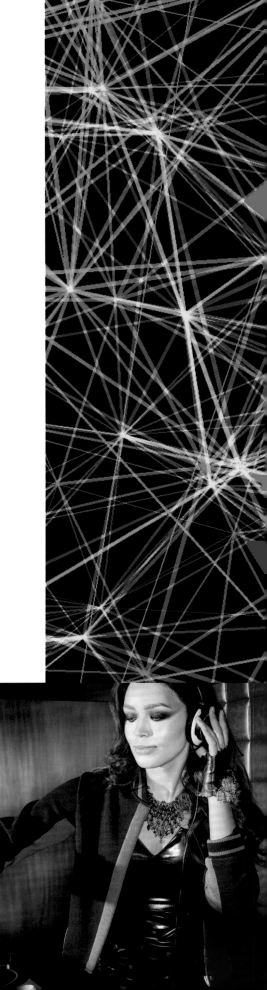

ELECTRIC FEEL

Wear the colors of the night.

"Too much is never enough, that is the motto of my family!"

Irina Volkonskii

The ultimate clubbing color combination is electric blue and black. It is hip, intriguing, and looks great in the light.

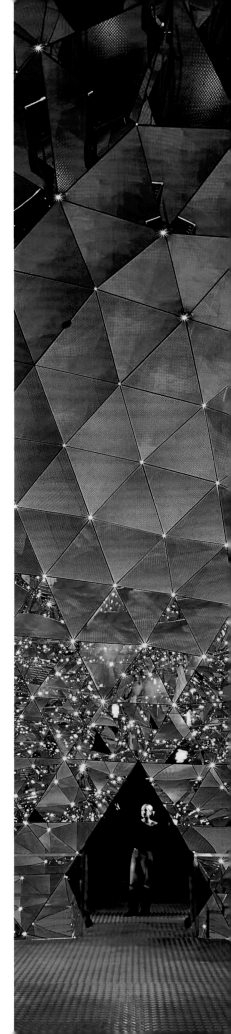

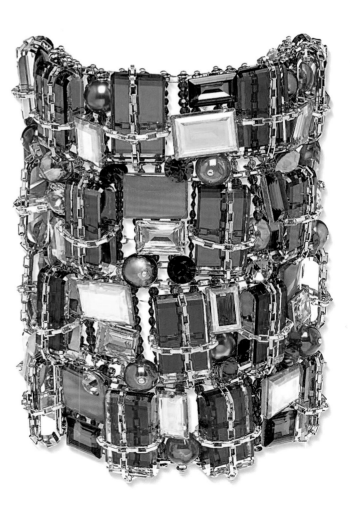

You have to be practical as you don't want your necklace to get caught in someone's mesh tee shirt while you dance, so choose complete, contained shapes. Tubular necklaces and resin beads are perfect for getting lost in music in style. If you really want to stand out, try a white resin necklace with metallic accents. Under regular lights, it will be a statement piece, but under the blue neon of a club, it will start to glow and become something totally different.

STRETCH THE SILHOUETTE

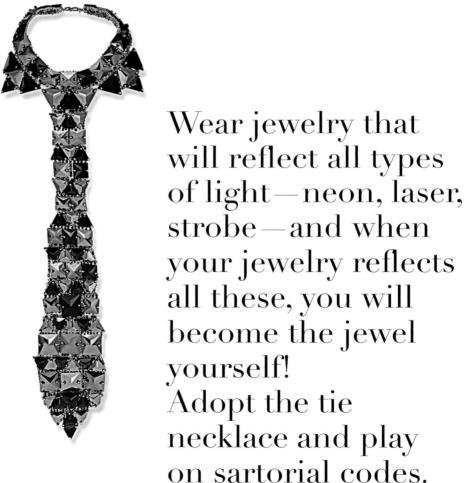

Take a different approach to jewelry, and add height to your figure by wearing tie necklaces. Don't be afraid to channel a more androgynous style.

Wear jewelry that will reflect all types of light—neon, laser, strobe—and when your jewelry reflects all these, you will become the jewel yourself! Adopt the tie necklace and play on sartorial codes.

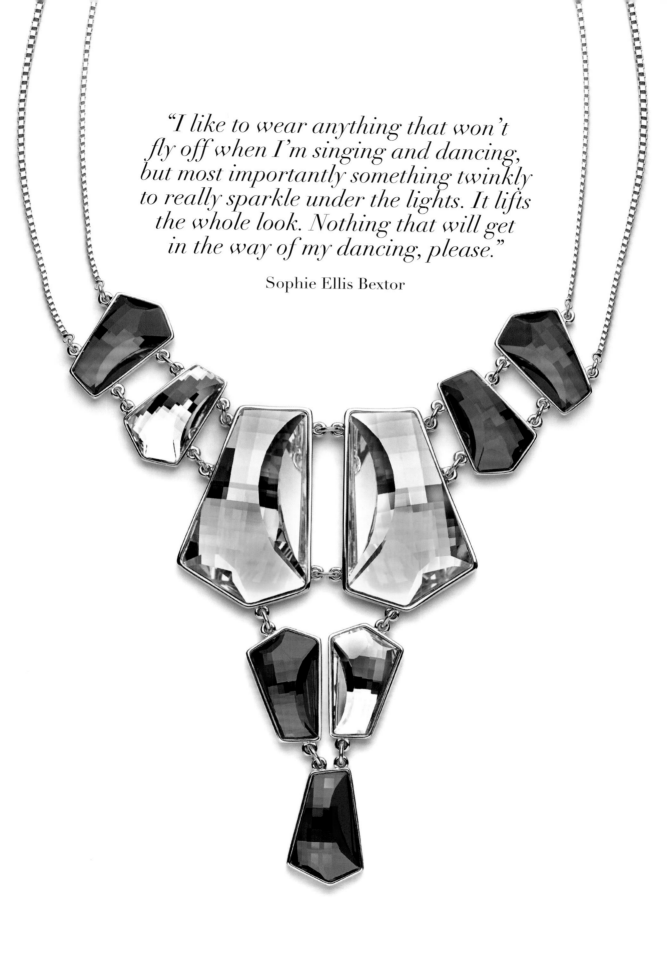

"I like to wear anything that won't fly off when I'm singing and dancing, but most importantly something twinkly to really sparkle under the lights. It lifts the whole look. Nothing that will get in the way of my dancing, please."

Sophie Ellis Bextor

READY
TO
ROCK

The room is quiet and you feel a breeze coming through the open window. You feel relaxed and know the day is all yours. You don't have to go to work, you don't have to do anything you don't want to do. The sheets feel soft on your skin. You turn around and fumble to turn on the stereo. You jump out of bed and you're soon trance dancing.

CUFFS CUFFS CUFFS

Rock 'n' roll style is about maximalism and excess. Choose large cuffs with chunky stones set in metal or resin.

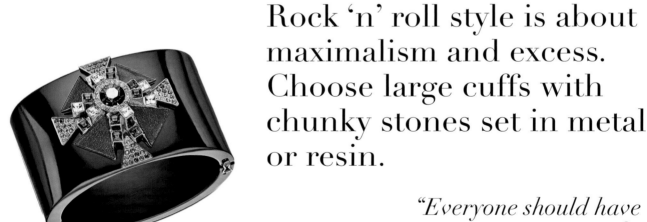

"Everyone should have a signature piece of jewelry and never take it off, even when they are asleep or in the bath. For me, it's my golden bangles. If you don't have one, get one!"

Han Huo Huo

Cuffs are powerful, both visually and because of their size. Some even have rings attached to them, making them a complete piece of jewelry in themselves.

SPIKES & LEATHER

Spikes and leather are something eyecatching. . . . They are the sugar and spice of rock chicks.

"*We believed that anything that was worth doing was worth overdoing.*"

Steven Tyler

Rock 'n' roll is about excess, exaggeration, individuality, irreverence, and fun... A lot of fun.

METALLIC CHAINS

Metallic chains are the ultimate rock 'n' roll signature look.

Whether made of silver, black ceramic or gunmetal, chains are your best asset if you fancy yourself as a rock chick. Choose bold, chunky chains, and wear lots at the same time!

BAROQUE OPULENCE

For the days you feel more glam rock than punk, try a touch of brocade and really ornate jewelry.

A torn heart is a classic goth symbol, reminiscent of Tim Burton movies and dark fairytales. If you really want to indulge your rebellious side, wear only one earring or if you feel particularly wild wear both earrings on the same ear.

"I am very sensitive to rock beats. Listening to Blondie, Beth Ditto, David Bowie, The Killers, Iggy Pop, The Doors . . . keeps my energy level high. Rock jewels also have that powerful energy, especially when combined with leather or lacquered outfits."

Nathalie Colin

NEO-GOTHIC SYMBOLS

Don't be afraid to make the most of goth imagery and symbolism.

Torn hearts, wings, skulls, crosses, and vintage cameos should all be part of your jewelry armada.

Your hair is wild, your feet won't stop moving. As you sway around the room, you grab a handful of bangles and put them on. They jangle to the beat of the drums. In your silk night dress, you imagine you are Debbie Harry. Still dancing, you put on your brightest lipstick, pausing only to pretend it's a microphone.

Right now, you could be David Bowie or Debbie Harry. You could even be PJ Harvey.

Men are simple creatures at heart and sometimes they need a little help. So use your clothes and accessories to point them in the right direction. Bear in mind that your best assets, such as a quick wit and a great sense of humor, don't need clothes to help them out, but you still want to enhance and make the most of your own physical assets.

A caged heart is a powerful symbol to wear for a rendezvous; it is also a sexy design in itself.

A choker designed to look like fishnet panty-hose is quite a talking point in an otherwise simple outfit.

SENSUAL LACE

Lace is the most sensual fabric. It evokes a frisson of excitement, it is intimate, and yet it reveals only a little while letting the imagination do the rest.

Chandelier earrings may not be your first choice when getting ready for a date, but they probably should be. . . .

Their fluidity and the way they follow the movements of your body will give you an extra special aura of sensuality. To avoid them looking too aggressive, pick pastel colors and mix pearls and stones.

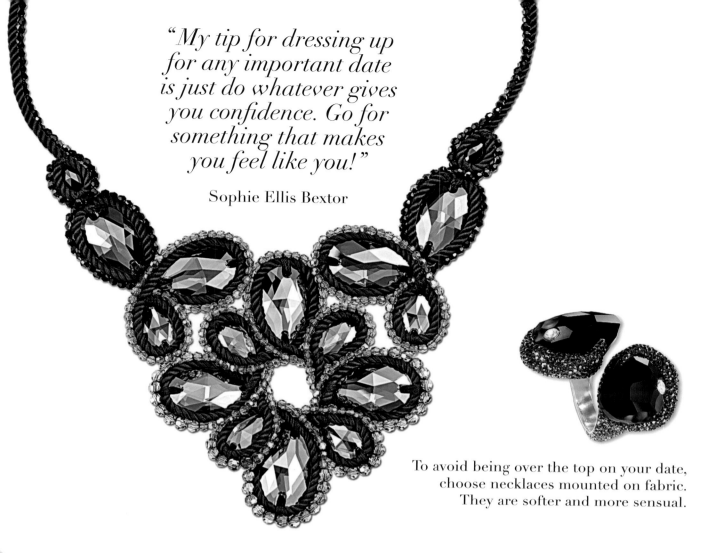

"My tip for dressing up for any important date is just do whatever gives you confidence. Go for something that makes you feel like you!"

Sophie Ellis Bextor

To avoid being over the top on your date, choose necklaces mounted on fabric. They are softer and more sensual.

If you have an elegant neck, wear your hair up and clip on some earrings so his eyes are drawn to it. If you are particularly proud of your cleavage, a rope necklace will work wonders, guiding his eyes down from your lips to your décolletage as you talk. Your eyes and your lips are your chief protagonists tonight!

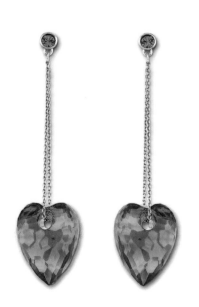

FETISH!

Avoid wearing too many metal bangles that will jangle each time
you move and rings
that will get caught
in unfortunate places.

Design by
Marek Wojcicki

195

"You don't want to show off too much and arrive covered in jewelry. You don't want the man of your dreams to think you are a high maintenance princess, at least not on the first date."

Nathalie Colin

CELEB

RATION

The festive season is the ideal time to bring out sequins, glitter, and all things metallic. Jewelry can be as sparkly as you like and the star is quite literally the star of the show. Stars around your neck, adorning your ears or mounted on a cuff all echo the Christmas star perched on top of the tree, symbolizing both high hopes and high ideals.

"A woman is taken into the world of dreams by dressing herself with the luminance of stars."

Tokujin Yoshioka

BRIGHT STARS

*"Celebrations are a good time to play
with things that glitter and sparkle,
adding a touch of light, joy, and
glamour. Radiant jewels, stars, gilt,
dangling briolettes, a rainbow of colors
. . . can all be combined with clothes in
festive fashion, but not necessarily in too
opulent a manner, as celebrations
are rather intimate occasions."*

Nathalie Colin

"Don't listen to rules about how to wear jewelry. Mixing different metals is a fun way to modernize any look. Just be creative and let the jewelry tell a story about who you are that day."

Lisa S.

METALLICS

Mix gold and silver for a 21st-century look. Contrast with matte leather as a novel touch.

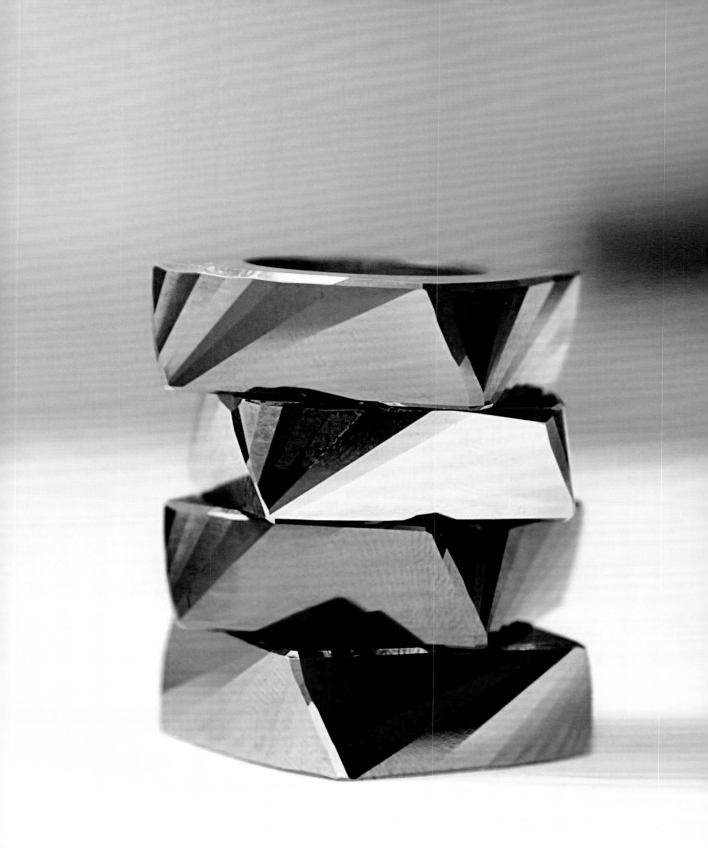

When it comes to festive jewelry, don't be afraid of mixing metals, but you can also go for a mono-metallic look, with a jacket of silver sequins accessorized with so many silver chains that it's hard to see where the jacket stops and the necklace starts. You can apply this rule anytime, don't feel you have to wait until December to try it out!

STATEMENT EARRINGS

Your hair length shouldn't define the type of earrings you wear. Statement earrings are for everyone, just don't combine them with a necklace.

"I don't have any strict rules for jewelry myself. But I try to remember the one that says "big earrings, no necklace, or big necklace, no earrings."

Stephanie Sigman

Christmas is not the only time of the year you have something to celebrate, think about all the occasions you can dress up and have fun in spring . . .
Don't stick to metallic jewelry when it comes to these, instead go for colorful, playful stones. Think of a luscious fruit salad, a candy store or a sparkling rainbow.

WED

DING

However different we are as individuals and however varied our lifestyles, our big day, the happiest of our life, can end up being very similar to everyone else's. Whether you like it or not, and even if you decide to shun social conventions, on your wedding day you are likely to end up wearing a dress of some description, accessorized with a big smile, and you will thank the makeup maestros for having invented the miracle of waterproof mascara!

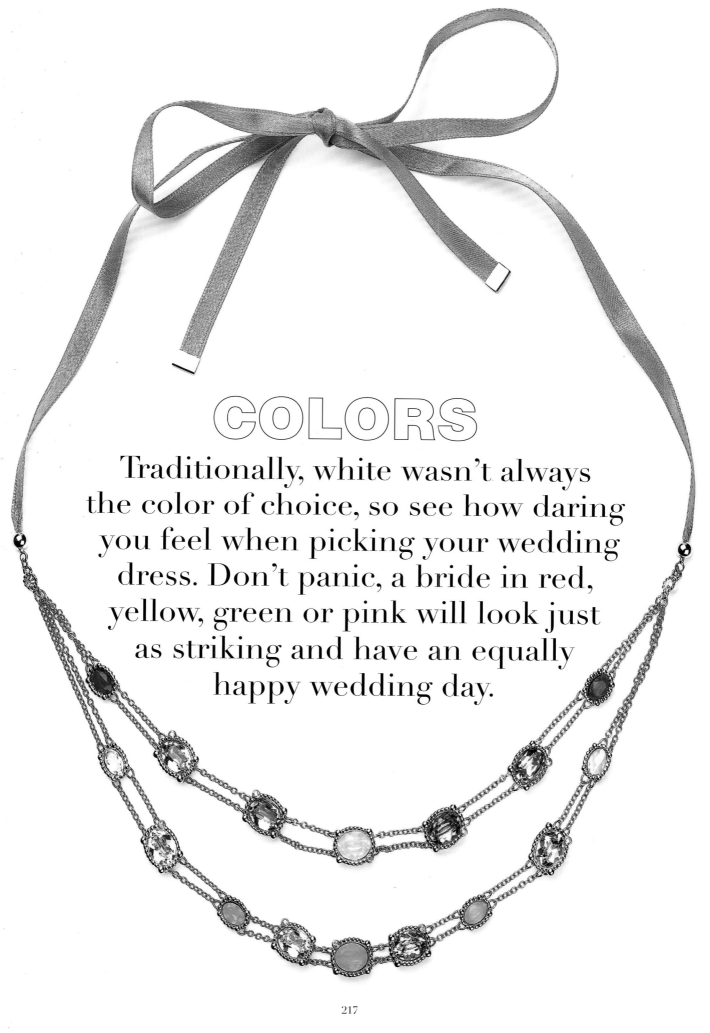

COLORS

Traditionally, white wasn't always the color of choice, so see how daring you feel when picking your wedding dress. Don't panic, a bride in red, yellow, green or pink will look just as striking and have an equally happy wedding day.

Just for now, let's assume you will be wearing white on your wedding day. Let's also assume that the main pieces of jewelry will be your engagement ring and the much anticipated simple gold band that will adorn your left hand in sickness and in health, till death do you part. You certainly don't want to wear too much jewelry but do accessorize your white dress.

"On my wedding day I want to wear jewels like talismans, so that my love life will be protected by every possible god, including the god of jewelry."

Nathalie Colin

"Earrings are the must-have jewelry item, because they emphasize your face and define its look. Earrings can even make up for makeup! With beautiful hair, showy earrings highlight the color of your eyes and your dress."

Anna dello Russo

ONE STATEMENT PIECE

Add a stylish touch to your dress with a large, unusual piece of jewelry.

Brides often worry about wearing too much jewelry in case it detracts from their wedding ring. This can happen, but if you wear a couture piece that is an ornate extension of your dress, it looks great.

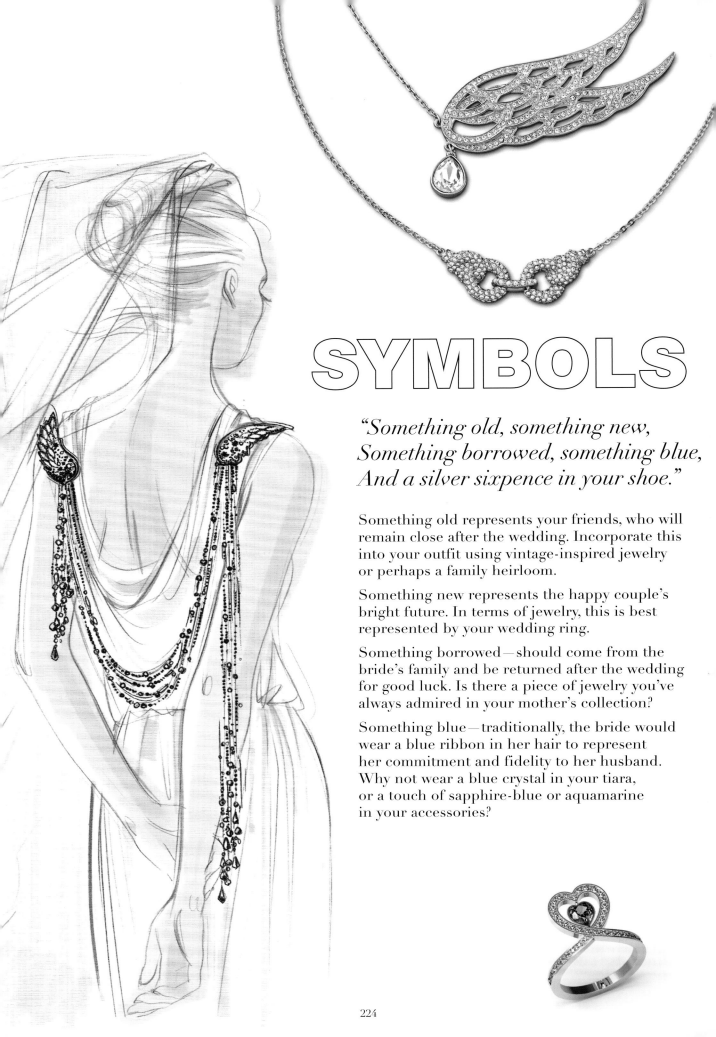

SYMBOLS

"Something old, something new,
Something borrowed, something blue,
And a silver sixpence in your shoe."

Something old represents your friends, who will remain close after the wedding. Incorporate this into your outfit using vintage-inspired jewelry or perhaps a family heirloom.

Something new represents the happy couple's bright future. In terms of jewelry, this is best represented by your wedding ring.

Something borrowed—should come from the bride's family and be returned after the wedding for good luck. Is there a piece of jewelry you've always admired in your mother's collection?

Something blue—traditionally, the bride would wear a blue ribbon in her hair to represent her commitment and fidelity to her husband. Why not wear a blue crystal in your tiara, or a touch of sapphire-blue or aquamarine in your accessories?

It's your wedding day so be as overt as you like. Go heavy on the symbolism.

A heart-shaped pendant on a plain silver chain, earrings with a wing motif, a simple silver or gold bangle with a knot twist. If you are feeling daring, dust off your tiara for a romantic glow under your veil.

"*The bride should choose a gown that reflects who she is before all else.*"

Vera Wang

FOR YOUR HAIR

If you want something a little more unconventional, forget the veil altogether and just wear a tiara.

Your wedding day is a truly joyous occasion and way up there on the list of happiest days of your life, but don't let it steal the thunder from all other occasions. Let it guide you toward a long, happy life together, where every day is worth celebrating. Dream, love, live, and, most of all, have fun, with or without jewelry!

"I imagine this book to be used in the way I use a cookery book. It is the basis for a few good recipes, but halfway through cooking your imagination takes over and this sense of freedom can create amazing outcomes and … even a few not quite so welcome surprises! But in fashion we have learnt to appreciate aesthetic accidents!"

Nathalie Colin

This very dear project has been possible with the immediate and strong support from Robert Buchbauer, Member of the Executive Board and Swarovski family member, who, as my superior has always given me the freedom and the necessary back-up to express my creative vision at Swarovski.

I also would like to thank my colleagues Joan Ng, Roland Moecke, Bernard Pleschko, Eric Schinzel, Arno Ebner and Jeffrey Howard, at CGB core management team, who have supported the original idea to come to fruition. Thousand "merci" to my team who has helped me produce the book, in particular my friend Yamila Tandeau de Marsac with her sharp creative talent and attention to details, Allison Pyrah for her valuable project lead across continents assisted by the enthusiastic Marjan Tharin.

Both legal and communication topics have been brilliantly taken care of, by Alison Lazerwitz and Hervé Delpech, together with Regina Arquint, François Ortarix, Celia Aklil, Sylvain Dao, Mary Lau, Livia Marotta just to name a few.

Last but not least, I enjoyed so much the photo-shoots and positive energy from Swarovski employees who took part by becoming supermodels for the day!

Thank you to our inspired guest stylists June Ambrose, Sascha Lilic and Han Huo Huo, as well as to the contributing photographers in particular the multi-talented Ralph Wenig, and glamorous models in NY, HK and Paris for their local interpretation of styling yourself with jewelry; Laetitia Wajnapel for turning my thoughts and styling tips into colorful words; and all the opinion leaders & personalities for their insightful generous quotations. And to Tinou Le Joly Senoville for her legendary coloristic talent, brilliantly helped for the crystal color ranges by Aurélie Jouan and Andelka Marjanovic for her precious contribution through this project.

I extend my sincere thanks to the team at La Martinière for believing in the project and helping me to shape the book. Thank you to those who will carry on the initial enthusiasm and take this project further by sharing it with the readers across the world.

And finally, thanks to my parents who have always nurtured my creative dreams, deep thanks to François for his sparkling love and always to my "crystalline" daughter Anh Ly, the jewel of my life.

SWAROVSKI

PHOTOGRAPHERS

Ezequiel de La Rosa
Noel Jones
Antoine Kralik
Mikocokiki
Emmanuel N'Guyen
Jean-Claude Roblique
Ralph Wenig - Artsphere

ILLUSTRATORS

Lea Dickely
Julie Lavayssière
Erin Petson
Linda Reinders
Pascaline Weiss

STYLISTS

June Ambrose
Han Huo Huo
Sascha Lilic

COLOR RANGE

Tinou Le Joly Sénoville

SWAROVSKI STAFF/SUPERMODELS FOR A DAY

Gwendoline Bella - Nora Bedjguelel - Hanne Bendixen - Jillian Castaldi - Sylvain Dao - Michiyo Deruelles
Arno Ebner - Bengt Jacobsson - Aurélie Jouan - Mary Lau - Daphné Laurent - Julie Lavayssière - Tiphaine Le Bourdais
Estelle Lebrun - Yelena Leshchinsky - Nadine Mao - Julia Mazenq - Deborah Mehmann - Caroline Meier - Lucia Nguyen
Lisabeta Petrisor - Allison Pyrah - Eva Reber - Simone Rossmann - Valérie Samuel - Carla Shanks - Guillemette Simpson
Yamila Tandeau de Marsac - Marjan Tharin - Makiko Weis - Jessica Wu

GUEST MODELS

Carole Dardanne
Tinou Le Joly Sénoville
Barbara Lepagnot
Francois Louis
Anh Ly Roblique
Brisa Roché
Nicolas Salomon
Yassen Samouilov from « on aura tout vu »
Justin Serigba
Livia Stoianova from « on aura tout vu »
Irina Volkonskii

WARDROBE CREDITS

PARIS ALEXIS MABILLE / ALICE BY TEMPERLEY / ALLIUMB / ANNE FONTAINE / AQUILANO RIMONDI / ARROW / AUSTIN REED / BRUNELLO CUCINELLI / CLUB MONACO / COMMUUN DANIEL HECHTER / DEVASTEE / DIM / DKNY / DROME / DSQUARED2 / FINE COLLECTION FOREVER 21 PINKO / G-STAR / GIANMARCO LORENZI / GINA SHOES / GIORGIO / GIUSEPPE ZANOTTI DESIGN / HENRY ARLINGTON / HÔTEL PARTICULIER / JEXIKA / JOIE / LANVIN LEONARD / LYDIA COURTEILLE / MAISON F / MOKUBA / N21 / NEW LOOK / NICHOLAS KIRKWOOD / PATRIZIA PEPE / RICHARD GAMPEL / SHIATZY CHEN / SMALTO / TATTY DEVINE TEMPERLEY / VERTIGO LIE SANG BONG / WOLFORD

NEW YORK ALEXANDER WANG / BALENCIAGA / BEBE / BURBERRY / CATHERINE MALANDRINO LOOK #15 / DIANE VON FURSTENBURG / EQUIPMENT / EREDAPPA / ETOILE BY ISABEL MARANT H&M / HALSTON / HAUTE HIPPIE / L.A.M.B. / MAISONETTE 1977 / MALOLES SHOES / MOSCHINO PATRICIA UNDERWOOD FOR CHRIS BENZ / PHILLIP LIM / SOSIE / SUNO / ZARA

HONG KONG BALMAIN / CHICTOPIA BY LIU QINGYANG / I.T / MASHA MA / ZARA

PHOTOGRAPHIC CREDITS

All crystal jewelry featured in the book is from Swarovski's past or present collections, with a selection from Atelier Swarovski, lola&grace, and Chamilia.

The Publisher and Swarovski would like to thank Laëtitia Casta, Yasmine Le Bon, Stephanie Sigman and Dita Von Tesse, and all the models and stylists who had collaborated on this book.

Printed and bound in Italy